W9-CDM-975

WITHDRAWN

PRIMARY SOURCES OF POLITICAL SYSTEMS™

SOCIALISM
A PRIMARY SOURCE ANALYSIS

JESSE JARNOW

rosen central
Primary Source™
The Rosen Publishing Group, Inc., New York

Published in 2005 by The Rosen Publishing Group, Inc.
29 East 21st Street, New York, NY 10010

Copyright © 2005 by The Rosen Publishing Group, Inc.

First Edition

All rights reserved. No part of this book may be reproduced in any form without permission in writing from the publisher, except by a reviewer.

Library of Congress Cataloging-in-Publication Data

Jarnow, Jesse.
Socialism: a primary source analysis / Jesse Jarnow.— 1st ed.
    p. cm. — (Primary sources of political systems)
Includes bibliographical references and index.
Contents: Introduction—The birth of socialism—Karl Marx, Friedrich Engels, and the communist manifesto—The industrial workers of the world and trade syndicalism—Paths of socialism—A new view of the world.
ISBN 0-8239-4521-9 (library binding)
1. Socialism. 2. Communism. [1. Socialism. 2. Communism.]
I. Title. II. Series.
HX40.J32 2004
335—dc22
                                                                    2003015898

Manufactured in the United States of America

On the cover: French president François Mitterrand *(standing, left)* participating in the traditional Bastille Day military parade on July 14, 1992.

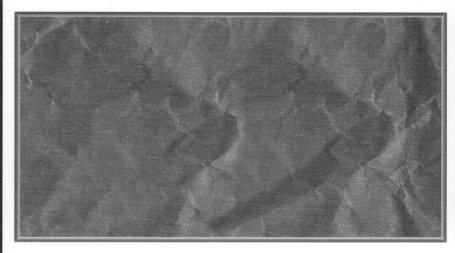

CONTENTS

Socialism is a political system in which the means of producing and distributing goods—land, labor, and capital—are owned collectively by the population and are controlled and managed by a central government. It evolved in Europe during the nineteenth century as a reaction to the excesses of the Industrial Revolution. At that time, wealth was concentrated in the hands of a few capitalists, or businesspeople, while industrial workers suffered significant economic hardships.

Early Socialists believed that the inequities of the Industrial Revolution would disappear if there were no businesspeople trying to make a profit. In addition, they embraced the idea that workers should have political power. This goal could be achieved if governments redistributed wealth from the capitalists to the workers. Socialists envisioned that such a system would lead to an end to poverty and, eventually, harmonious societies of equals. In these societies, cooperation, rather than competition, would drive economic activity. There would be no rich, no poor, no sick, no hungry.

Europe's ruling classes resented this radical idea of Socialism. Karl Marx and Friedrich

Clement Attlee (1883–1967), leader of the British Labour Party, addresses demonstrators at a rally in Cardiff, Great Britain, on August 2, 1936. Attlee was one of the most prominent British Socialists of the twentieth century.

Engels, who can fairly be described as two of the main architects of Socialism, noted this in *The Communist Manifesto*. They wrote, "A spectre is haunting Europe—the specter of Communism. All the Powers of old Europe have entered into a holy alliance to exorcise this spectre." The notion of power and wealth in the hands of the working class was frightening to the ruling classes especially because it would come at their expense.

In 1848, when Marx and Engels wrote *The Communist Manifesto*, Communism was more or less interchangeable with Socialism. Today, however, they are seen as different systems. The distinction between the two, though, is a little tricky and can be interpreted as a matter of degree. While both systems are rooted in the collective ownership of the means of production, Communism tends to be more totalitarian, or controlling, of nearly all aspects of society and individual rights. Control is often brought about by revolution and bloodshed. Socialism is more gradual and its goals are realized by winning elections and passing Socialist laws. Therefore, all Communists are Socialists, but not all Socialists are Communists. In short, Communism is an extreme form of Socialism.

Many countries experimented with Socialism during much of the twentieth century. Their governments sought to cash in on the Socialist theory that held that state ownership of industries allows for a central planner, the government, to use resources in a rational way to maximize efficiency and guarantee the economic welfare of the entire population. However, by the late twentieth century, the evidence of failed state after failed state made it clear that state ownership and planned economies were not very efficient. As a result, there has been a general movement away from Socialism toward capitalism over the last twenty years.

Like all major political systems, Socialism has never been practiced in its pure form. But unlike most of the other major systems, Socialism has widely come to be viewed as being unattainable or unsustainable on a large scale, as in the economic organization of a country. This does not mean, however, that Socialism is dead. It remains attractive to many developing countries where the gap between rich and poor is staggering. It also survives in large industrial, capitalist countries, including the United States, in policies—for example, welfare—that are intended to address the economic inequities of capitalism.

CHAPTER ONE

THE BIRTH OF SOCIALISM

There were three main precedents to the birth of Socialism: the ideas of Charles Fourier, Henri de Saint-Simon, and Robert Owen. Each came in the wake of sweeping changes wrought by Britain's Industrial Revolution starting in the mid-eighteenth century.

Efficient factories changed the way people worked, which, in turn, changed the way people lived. Where skilled artisans had previously manufactured the bulk of the world's goods by hand, machines such as automatic looms were beginning to take their places. Seeking employment, people flocked to cities. A new poverty emerged in factory

Robert Owen (1771–1858) was a labor reformer whose innovations inspired changes in British labor laws. He was a pioneer of British Socialism.

towns. If factories were making more products better and faster than before, then why were so many people living under such horrible conditions? The Industrial Revolution created new problems that would need solutions.

Utopians and Early Socialists

The men and women who tried to tackle these problems were called utopians. They looked for ways to turn the world into a utopia, or paradise—or, barring that, a better, more humane place. Their ideas were often far-fetched. However, there were some that were worth exploring.

Three men—Charles Fourier, Henri de Saint-Simon, and Robert Owen—had vastly different solutions to the problems the Industrial Revolution presented. Fourier and Saint-Simon were French. Owen was Welsh. What separated the three men from other utopians was the way their versions of utopia related to the modern world.

Industry was expanding. There was an ever-increasing gap between factory owners and factory workers. The new Socialists suggested that people who worked in the factories might own them as well. This fundamental change in approach rippled outward. The utopians began to envision new ways to structure society. Unlike previous utopian thinkers, the new utopians attempted to achieve a paradise that had little to do with religion. Everything they needed was before them.

This 1820 engraving depicts the Scottish village of New Lanark. New Lanark was established by Robert Owen in 1800. It was the successful realization of Owen's vision of an integrated cooperative community in which the welfare of citizens matched—and was even fostered by—the goal of commercial profit.

Robert Owen

Robert Owen was born in 1771 in Wales. By the time he was nineteen, he was the superintendent of a cotton mill. His work there resulted in the development of his radical worldview.

Owen was an atheist, someone who does not believe in God. He believed that a person's destiny was his or her own. People had to change their attitudes in order to succeed in life. A psychological revolution was needed, he said. Better environments would make for better people. He outlined his ideas in a book called *A New View of Society* (1813), in which he advocated small, self-sufficient communities.

Owen had a chance to test his theories in the Scottish town of New Lanark. In 1800, he set up a model factory and a model village. He made sure that working and living conditions were excellent. Owen paid special attention to education. The factory's earnings funded the school. New Lanark was a wild success. The factory turned a huge profit. More important, the workers were happy. Owens established many reforms at his factory. While most workers in England worked thirteen or fourteen hours a day, the men and women in Owen's factory worked only ten and a half hours.

Owen's financial backers thought he was spending too much money. They wanted less money put back into the community and more money given to the investors. Eventually, Owen broke his ties with them. He founded several other cooperative communities throughout Great Britain and one in the United States. None of them were as successful as New Lanark. Although Owen's communities eventually failed, he had a positive effect on the country's working conditions. From 1802 to 1891, the British parliament passed eight Factory Acts based on Owen's ideas.

Henri de Saint-Simon

Meanwhile, in France, Henri de Saint-Simon was championing his own ideas. Born in 1760, Saint-Simon fought alongside American colonists in the Revolutionary War (1775–1783). He made a small fortune in

This portrait of utopian Socialist Henri de Saint-Simon was created around 1790. Saint-Simon envisioned a system in which the state, led by businessmen, would manage the production and distribution of goods, establish a national community based upon cooperation, and eliminate poverty.

investments during the French Revolution. He celebrated the triumph of industry. Science, he thought, should guide society. It should aid religion, not replace it. He imagined that scientists and industrialists would be the leaders of the new society.

Saint-Simon wrote a number of essays, which are today collected in *Social Organization, the Science of Man and Other Writings*. In addition to his theory about the relationship between science and industry, he predicted a world in which politics and economics were joined. In the past fifty years, this has come to be true. However, it has not happened in the way Saint-Simon would have liked. He thought economic leaders could carefully plan production for the good of the people. The goal was not profit but harmony.

Gradually, he developed a cult of followers. As a movement, the Saint-Simonians advocated many of the causes that more mature forms of Socialism would embrace. They wished to abolish inheritance rights. They believed that workers should control the means of production and that women should be given more rights under the law. The Saint-Simonians were never able to put their theory into practice. After Saint-Simon died in 1825, the movement deteriorated into a religious cult. It soon succumbed to petty bickering and dissolved.

Charles Fourier

Perhaps the most influential of the early Socialists was Charles Fourier (1772–1837). He was easily the most optimistic (if most unrealistic) of the eighteenth-century Socialists. Like Saint-Simon, Fourier was French. He witnessed the French Revolution firsthand from his home in the provinces. He saw what industrialization had done to society. Unlike Saint-Simon, he did not embrace science and industry. He thought that by being forced into menial tasks, workers were becoming less able to think and reason.

Fourier presented a complete and exacting model for a new society, down to the most microscopic details. He planned different jobs for each member of his society, attempting to balance them carefully. Many historians believe he was a little crazy. Still, they consider him to be one of Socialism's most alluring figures. His *Theory of Social Organization*, published in 1820, was a massive work. It revealed the inner workings of a brilliant, if troubled, mind.

Fourier's work centered on his fervent belief in what he called Universal Analogy. Everything was connected, he thought. The physical world was an exact representation of the physical and spiritual laws of the universe, and everything reflected human nature. Fourier believed that his work logically followed Sir Isaac Newton's laws of gravitation. While Newton showed why physical objects are attracted to each other, Fourier attempted to do the same with the human spirit.

Fourier formulated his theory of attraction based on a detailed list of distinct personality types comprised of passions. His theory outlined twelve passions that must be satisfied for people to be happy. To attain this, he suggested a precise arrangement of personality types that would counterbalance each other. When this formula was followed, Fourier believed, harmony would be created within the universe. He called his paradise Harmony. Fourier planned to accomplish this through a series of communities called phalanxes.

Each phalanx would be a rigorously planned community. To Fourier, if people enjoyed their work, they would do it well. Jobs would be assigned based on the passions. Everything would fall into place around this. Fourier believed in his theories with an unwavering faith. He attracted his share of followers, though they were never able to raise the money to build an actual phalanx.

Fourier spent many years searching for financial backers. The broad scope of Fourier's project confused many potential followers. Where they were likely to be excited by one of his ideas, they were equally likely to be put off by others.

Many of Fourier's writings about Harmony closely resembled science fiction. Once the world adopted his systems, he believed, the average life span would increase to 144 years and humans would develop tails. The polar ice caps would melt, and the seas around

TWENTIETH-CENTURY KIBBUTZIM

Many have argued that Socialism would work on a small scale. Throughout much of the twentieth century, this was proved mostly true by a network of kibbutzim in Israel. A kibbutz is a small collective settlement. Residents live under communal principles. They divide the work equally and share larger possessions (such as cars). The average kibbutz has several hundred inhabitants. The population of the original kibbutz was generally made up of a combination of young Israelis, traveling students, and transient workers. Some have said that the kibbutzim are the closest that people have come to living the principles laid out by Charles Fourier. To others, kibbutzim feel very much like summer camps with more chores.

The first kibbutz was founded in 1910. After 1948, kibbutzim played an important part in the settlement of

A group of women plowing a field on a kibbutz in Israel around 1935.

continued on page 16

continued from page 15

Israel, forming the basis of small autonomous communities. For the most part, they are self-sufficient. The kibbutzim are bound together into several loose networks. Each kibbutz is arranged like a village. There is a library, a grocery, a laundry, and other services. There are few cars, and most residents walk or ride bicycles. Politically, a kibbutz is a direct democracy. Every member has a vote in each policy decision. Small committees deal with day-to-day planning on a variety of matters.

The residents of a kibbutz do a wide range of jobs. They are responsible for maintaining the settlement by doing chores. Kibbutzim make up an important part of Israel's agricultural output. Members harvest food for both themselves and others. Many kibbutzim also have industrial components to them. They manufacture a variety of products in small factories, including electric motors, irrigation systems, and clothing. Kibbutzim exist within a larger capitalist system. In recent years, this has led kibbutzim to change and evolve. There is more of an emphasis on the individual now. But, for the most part, kibbutzim retain their basic principles. The kibbutz still takes care of the housing, food, health care, and education of its inhabitants. Likewise, the means of production are still owned and controlled by the workers. Many kibbutzim supplement their incomes by offering bed-and-breakfast hotels. Many also have museums.

the North Pole would be turned into "a kind of lemonade." Man's enemies in the animal kingdom would become his allies, turning into such creatures as anticrocodiles and antisharks.

In short, Charles Fourier lived in a dream world. But it was a dream that ultimately had a positive effect on many people. Almost forty years after Fourier's death in 1837, Friedrich Engels wrote of him lovingly in *Socialism: Utopian and Scientific*, calling his work "masterly."

Owen, Saint-Simon, and Fourier provided the starting point for Karl Marx and Friedrich Engels's plans for widespread Socialist change. But where Marx and Engels would eventually call for statewide revolution, Owen, Saint-Simon, and Fourier favored small settlements. It was easier, they thought, to deal with a more controlled group of people. In this way, they were direct influences on hundreds of utopian communes and compounds that were founded across the globe. (A commune is a small community, usually based around a farm. People who live there share possessions and jobs.)

Brook Farm, Massachusetts

In 1841, George Ripley (1802–1880) founded Brook Farm in Massachusetts. He based his community on a combination of teachings of Fourier and the American writer and philosopher Henry David Thoreau. Likewise, a direct line can be drawn from Fourier, Owen, and Saint-Simon to the kibbutz movement in Israel. In the 1960s and 1970s, communes became quite popular in the

George Ripley was an ordained minister, social reformer, and writer. He enjoyed some success with Brook Farm, until a fire threw the project into financial ruin.

United States. Many idealistic young men and women moved to communes to escape the pressures of modern life. In industrialized nations, one buys food and clothing in stores. Those who moved to communes wanted to escape that. They wanted to be self-sufficient. For example, they wanted to grow their own food and sew their own clothes. In a sense, they agreed with Fourier. They wanted to be active in all aspects of their lives, not just their highly specialized jobs. Though most of the communes disbanded after several years, many still thrive.

CHAPTER TWO

Karl Marx, Friedrich Engels, and *The Communist Manifesto*

In the second half of the nineteenth century, life for many people in Europe worsened. Poverty continued to grow. There was great unrest among all classes. Socialism's popularity grew as well, as it appeared in society through a variety of outlets. Fourier had been a utopian. He was opposed to capitalism, an economic system based on private ownership. A new breed of thinkers soon emerged. They were the scientific Socialists. Among the leaders of this new movement were Karl Marx (1818–1883) and Friedrich Engels (1820–1895).

Marx was a German historian. Engels was born in Prussia

Friedrich Engels was the cofounder of modern Socialism and Communism. He wrote his first major work, *Conditions of the Working Class in England*, in 1844, months before he met Karl Marx.

Karl Marx is widely acknowledged as the principal architect of Socialism. The son of a German lawyer, he studied law, history, and philosophy before becoming the political editor of a radical German newspaper. The word "Marxism" is used to describe the social theory that is based on his writings.

(modern Germany), the son of a textile magnate. When he was young, Engels went to England to help his father manage his business. While he was there, he observed the conditions of the towns, the factories, and the people. He published his findings in a book. Shortly after, he began to write for a magazine that Marx edited. In 1844, in Paris, the two met in person. They began a relationship that would last until Marx died in 1883.

Marx and Engels belonged to the Communist League. In the nineteenth century, the word "Communist" meant something vastly different from what it came to imply later. For Marx and Engels, "Communism" and "Socialism" were interchangeable terms. So it was in 1847, when they drafted one of the most influential political documents in modern history, *The Communist Manifesto*.

The Communist Manifesto

The Communist Manifesto was divided into four parts. The first two of these are the most important. Part one outlines Marx and Engels's conception of history. Part two explains their plan for the present. Part three presents a detailed catalog of different kinds of Socialism. Finally, part four closes with a brief summary of the world situation and an enthusiastic call to arms.

This is a reproduction of the cover of the first English translation of *The Communist Manifesto*. The book was called the *Manifesto of the Communist Party* when this edition was published in London, England, in 1888. Refer to page 55 for a transcription of an excerpt.

Class Struggle

Marx and Engels emphasized teleology, the belief that history was working inevitably toward a final product. All of history, they said, was the result of class struggle between those who labored and those who con-trolled labor. Under feudalism, vassals and serfs worked in exchange for land and protection from lords. It was a highly controlled system. Men could not work for themselves.

This illustration, entitled *Propriétaire des choses* (The Properties of Things), depicts a feudal lord giving instructions to serfs under his protection. It appeared in a fifteenth-century manuscript called *Moeurs et usage* (Manners and Education). Serfs did most of the work in feudal society. They were bound to the land on which they worked.

Capitalism

Feudalism gave way naturally to capitalism, in which men were free to conduct business any way they wanted. If people worked for themselves, productivity was bound to increase. Free competition would lead to monopoly, Marx and Engels suggested. Monopolies would lead to price-fixing in which consumers would pay more for goods and services. What would begin with the ideal of complete freedom would perversely end with corporate totalitarianism and consolidation of companies. With this prediction, Marx and Engels were absolutely right. It occurred again and again in their day and continues to happen today.

Consolidation

Marx and Engels believed that this consolidation would also be capitalism's downfall. There would be a much greater gap between the classes. The factory owners who controlled the means of production were known as the bourgeoisie. The workers who toiled in factories were known as the proletariat. As time went on, the rich would get richer and the poor would get poorer.

However, the proletariat was now relatively centralized since its members all worked in factories. They would organize by forming unions and workers' organizations. And, once they were organized, they would overthrow the bourgeoisie.

Revolution

Marx and Engels began to call for the revolution that they thought was inevitable. In their world, the idea of revolution was not so

Dystopian Literature

A dystopia is the opposite of a utopia. If a utopia is a perfect world, then a dystopia is an imperfect world. There is a wide body of dystopian novels and films. Most of them are set in either the future or alternate versions of the present. They depict dark versions of the world under oppressive totalitarian governments. Many are fantasies written as if history made a different turn at an important juncture. Philip K. Dick's *The Man in the High Castle* (1962), for example, imagined what would happen if the United States had lost World War II (1939–1945).

The most common plot in dystopian literature is that of a single man's battle against a dehumanizing society. Some of the more popular works include George Orwell's *1984* (1949), Aldous Huxley's *Brave New World* (1932), Ray Bradbury's *Fahrenheit 451* (1953), and Franz Kafka's *The Trial* (1925). These books were all quite controversial. People were scared by their implications because the books took negative elements of modern society and magnified them.

The works grew out of Socialism in several ways. The authors were attempting to answer many of the same questions that Karl Marx faced. They raised important issues about an individual's place in society. They considered what contribution a person should make. They pondered the role of the government. In the process, they critiqued both Socialism and capitalism. If pushed to their extremes, Socialism and capitalism resembled each other in their Fascism. That is, if you work out Socialism to its extreme (total governmental control of all public works), it is quite similar to what capitalism is when worked out to its extreme (consolidation by several large corporations that own everything). The books revealed the similar human impulses behind both systems.

There is a wicked sense of humor behind much dystopian literature and film. Terry Gilliam's film *Brazil* (1985) is a darkly hilarious look at a totalitarian regime. In this world, for example, it is illegal for one to fix his or her own plumbing. The government technicians who have permission to make the repairs must fill out an array of official paperwork to do so.

While the mix of social criticism and humor can make many readers and viewers uncomfortable, it serves an important purpose. Often more disturbing than funny, these works encourage people to take a closer look at the world in which they live. Dystopian works push readers to value and protect the freedoms they have by showing them what life would be like without them.

far-fetched. Fifty years earlier, a series of revolts had taken place in France. Only three years before, weavers in Germany had attacked the homes of factory owners. Living conditions were horrible. Famines occurred throughout Europe, driving up food prices. In some cities, there were riots over the high costs of bread and potatoes. Meanwhile, wages dropped to an all-time low. If there was any time and place ripe for revolution, it was Europe in the mid-nineteenth century.

Rethinking Society

In *The Communist Manifesto*, Marx and Engels outlined the specifics of what they wanted to achieve. Their goals ranged from personal to governmental. Like Saint-Simon, they believed that a change in society could come only with a broad shift in thinking. They wanted to liberate society from the psychological shackles imposed on it by capitalism.

The first step, they wrote, was universal suffrage. Everybody should have the right to vote, from people of the proletariat to members of the bourgeoisie. In addition, Marx and Engels wished to ban private property. By "private property" they did not mean personal goods but, rather, property on a larger scale, such as factories. Industry would be placed in the hands of the government. And, with the government (theoretically) controlled by the people, it would enter the Socialist stage. Eventually, they predicted, mechanisms of the old class tensions would fall away, and a true Communist (or classless) state would be achieved. In nondemocratic countries, they called for revolution. "Working men of the world, unite!" they wrote.

Tireless Writers

Marx and Engels worked hard to present their vision to the world. They traveled the world, making speeches and helping workers organize. Both men also wrote a great deal. Because they wished to convert the world to their vision, they analyzed the world's current situation as well as its history.

In 1864, Marx addressed a conference in London at which the International Workingmen's Association was founded. Also known as the First International, it was an international organization that set out to bring together political groups and trade union organizations that were based on the working class.

In 1867, Marx published *Das Kapital* (Capital). It was the first of a proposed three volumes that would present his critique of capitalism. Unfortunately, Marx died in 1883, before he could complete the second and third volumes. Engels wrote two more volumes of *Das Kapital* and continued to edit Marx's work (as well as his own) until his death in 1895.

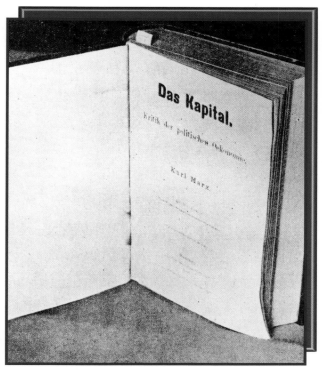

Das Kapital, Karl Marx's stinging criticism of capitalism, is widely seen to be Marx's most significant writing. The title page of the first edition is pictured here. Refer to page 55 for a translation of an excerpt from the book.

In the Footsteps of Marx and Engels

There has never been a fully functional example of Marx and Engels's vision. Several countries claimed to be Socialist, including the former

Soviet Union, though they weren't. In each case, governments took some elements of Socialism while disregarding its fundamental aspects. They twisted them into varieties of totalitarianism.

While Marx and Engels's brand of Socialism was never truly instituted, *The Communist Manifesto* spread throughout the world. It was translated into dozens of languages. It found its way into the hands of thousands of workers, organizers, and scholars, having perhaps a larger impact on the shape of world history than any other political document of modern times. Marx and Engels also inspired the founding of many Socialist parties and labor unions across Europe in the late nineteenth century. In turn, these would influence many social movements of the twentieth century.

CHAPTER THREE

THE COMMUNIST STRAIN

This photograph shows construction workers building a giant tractor plant in Belorussia, USSR. The plant was part of Joseph Stalin's efforts to industrialize the Soviet Union under his Five Year Plan.

The Union of Soviet Socialist Republics (USSR) came closest to achieving Socialism on a large scale. It was formed in 1922 under the direction of Russian premier Vladimir Ilyich Lenin (1870–1924). It began as a confederation of six nations: Russia, Ukraine, Georgia, Azerbaijan, Armenia, and Belarus. It later grew into a sprawling empire consisting of fifteen republics.

The Birth of Soviet Socialism

Five years before, in 1917, Lenin rose to power in Russia following the October Revolution during which his Bolshevik Party overthrew the government. Once in power, Lenin abolished private ownership of land and began distributing confiscated land among the peasants. He placed workers in control of factory production. He also nationalized banks and large companies. In other words, he placed them under government ownership and control.

Lenin's government faced wide resistance from Russians who resented both the way he seized power and his policies. The resistance escalated into a civil war which lasted four years. During the civil war, Lenin introduced a program called War Communism. Under this program, the government nationalized all companies. In doing so, it determined what would be produced. It also had the power to force people to work in certain industries. The government also required farmers to turn over grain and vegetables to soldiers upon request. The policies of War Communism also wiped out many of the freedoms that Russians had won in the wake of the October Revolution. Meanwhile, Lenin used his private army to suppress his opposition. The government was ruthless in silencing its critics.

Beyond the force of Lenin's oppression, the effects of War Communism had a devastating effect on the Russian population. Food shortages and famine were widespread, and many people died from starvation. Many peasants rioted and participated in strikes and demonstrations in protest.

Under pressure, Lenin was forced to reconsider some of his policies. In 1921, he announced his New Economic Policy, which relaxed some of his restrictions on private ownership. Within months, the shift in economic policies began to bear fruit. Russia's system of food distribution improved to the benefit of the peasants. By the end of the year, Lenin had brutally silenced his political opponents

U.S. president Warren Harding organized the American Relief Administration to distribute food and seed grains within several famine-stricken regions of Russia in 1921. The famine was one of the consequences of the Russian civil war. This photograph shows American volunteers distributing relief supplies to Russian peasants.

and Russia was totally under his control. Lenin's Bolshevik Party changed its name to the Communist Party. It became the only recognized political organization in the USSR. The Communist Party ruled as a dictatorship by decree. The New Economic Policy was still in force when Lenin died in 1924.

The USSR Under Joseph Stalin

Vladimir Lenin *(left)* and Joseph Stalin were the first two leaders of the Soviet Union. Shortly before he died, Lenin wrote an article advising the Communist Party to remove Stalin from his powerful position as general secretary. Stalin suppressed the article after Lenin's death.

Lenin's death set off a power struggle within the Communist Party. In the end, Joseph Stalin (1879–1953) seized control of the party and of the Soviet Union. He immediately set out to eliminate his rivals and all potential opposition to his leadership. Within a decade, he was the unquestioned leader of both the Communist Party and the Soviet Union.

Almost immediately, Stalin set out to transform the Soviet Union into a completely Socialist state. Accordingly, in 1927, he canceled Lenin's New Economic Policy. In 1928, he introduced his first Five Year Plan. It was a sweeping economic policy that had two main goals: industrialization and collectivization. Stalin set out to quickly transform the Soviet Union into an industrialized nation and consolidate the nation's small, individual farms into a sweeping system of large nationalized farms.

Under the Five Year Plan, all industry and services were nationalized. Central planners set strict output quotas for factories. New plants and industrial centers were developed, especially in heavy industries such as iron and steel and machinery.

In agriculture, the government put the nation's farms under state control. Unfortunately, the farmers were often made to serve the interests of the army and the cities at the expense of rural residents. Members of the collective farms were not allowed any grain until the government's high quotas were met. Those who broke the rules faced stiff punishment. This put an undue strain on the country's farmers, who didn't have enough to eat. In Ukraine, the strict enforcement of collectivization led to the famine of 1932 to 1933. Between 6 and 7 million people died as a result.

By 1940, after a number of five year plans, roughly 97 percent of all peasant households were incorporated into collective farms.

This memorandum from the Central Committee of the Communist Party of Ukraine outlines punitive measures it has decided to take against several villages. The villages were not cooperating with the state-mandated grain collection. Refer to page 56 for a transcription of the memo.

This photograph shows Russian exiles in Siberia. From as early as the seventeenth century, Russian rulers have used Siberia as a place of exile and forced labor camps for political enemies. Lenin, Stalin, and later Soviet dictators continued the practice. Communist regimes also used Siberia to conduct secret research, including the testing of weapons of mass destruction.

Loss of Civil Liberties

Stalin's government was ruthless and cruel, frequently murdering those who dared to dissent. While the country was, in fact, socialized, it was never placed in the hands of the proletariat. There were some positive aspects to the socialization of the Soviet Union.

Literacy rates improved significantly. Medical coverage became almost universal. Unfortunately, these came at great human expense.

The government controlled production and the media. The right to dissent was quashed. This is one of the primary problems of large-scale Socialism. Not everyone wants to participate, and the Soviet Union was particularly forceful. Many of those who resisted were sent to labor camps in Siberia. Nevertheless, collectivization helped Stalin achieve his other goal of industrialization. By the time Stalin died in 1953, the USSR had been catapulted into a global superpower.

The Spread of Communism

Through military and diplomatic means, Stalin oversaw the spread of Communism throughout Eastern Europe and Asia. He helped bring Communist governments to power in Albania, Bulgaria, Hungary, Poland, Romania, and Yugoslavia between 1944 and 1947.

Stalin's successors also worked to spread Communism throughout the world. As had happened in the USSR, the Communist revolutions created individual dictatorships rather than dictatorships of the proletariat. Instead of workers' committees influencing policy and selecting leaders, power was concentrated in the hands of a few, whose decrees were brutally imposed on the population.

It soon became clear that Communism in practice verged far from Marx's theories. It had become a severe strain on the very people whose rights it was supposed to defend. Eventually, the strain became unbearable. In 1991, after years of economic and military standoffs with the West, led by the United States, Communism collapsed in the Soviet Union.

CHAPTER FOUR

DEMOCRATIC SOCIALISM

To Marx and Engels, Socialism and Communism were basically synonymous. But as the Communist movement grew, it soon became clear that there was a division between those who insisted that the Communist revolution had to be forced through violent means and those who felt that it could be achieved through the democratic process. The differences between the two groups widened once the world had seen the Soviet experiment.

In the years following World War II, Socialists around the world reconsidered their positions. The world had changed dramatically. The failures of the Communist

Pierre Trudeau served as Canada's prime minister from April 20, 1968, to June 3, 1979 and from March 3, 1980, to June 30, 1984. Under Trudeau, the national budget and the size and power of the government bureaucracy grew significantly.

Soviet Union were clear. So were the successes of the capitalist United States.

At a convention held in Frankfurt, Germany, in 1951, Socialist International, an umbrella association of international Socialist organizations, further distanced itself from Communism. It did so in a document that has become known as the Frankfurt Declaration. It said, in part:

> Since the Bolshevik revolution in Russia, Communism has split the International Labour Movement and has set back the realisation of Socialism in many countries for decades. Communism falsely claims a share in the Socialist tradition. In fact it has distorted that tradition beyond recognition. It has built up a regid theology which is incompatable with the critical spirit of Marxism . . . Wherever it has gained power it has destroyed freedom or the chance of gaining freedom.

The document also outlined the general goals of Socialism and reinforced the major themes that Marx and Engels had established in *The Communist Manifesto*.

> Socialism aims to liberate the peoples from dependence on a minority which owns or controls the means of production. It aims to put economic power in the hands of the people as a whole, and to create a community in which free men work together as equals.

In 1956, British scholar C. A. R. Crosland wrote an important book titled *The Future of Socialism*. The book evaluated Socialism's goals and compared them to the current state of the world.

C. A. R. Crosland's *The Future of Socialism* was a major influence on the British Labour Party after World War II. Between 1950 and 1977, when he died, he was a member of Parliament. He also held various cabinet positions in several Labour Party administrations.

Socialism in the Twentieth Century

Socialism's main goal in the early twentieth century, Crosland wrote, was to create a welfare state. By that, he meant a government that would provide for and support its citizens. Looked at from that perspective, Crosland said, Socialists had accomplished quite a lot. However, there were still several objectives yet to be achieved. Of prime importance was the diffusion of power. The upper class still dominated most countries. In addition, the standard of living needed to be raised.

The British Labour Party

Crosland was a member of the Labour Party. The party was founded in 1900 as the parliamentary wing of Britain's trade union movement. It rose to prominence in the 1940s and 1950s. Crosland and his associates advocated a less revolutionary way of achieving Socialist aims within a government. They were inspired by U.S. president Franklin Delano Roosevelt's sweeping social programs in America, many of which had been dismantled during World War II. As the Labour Party came to power in Britain over the course of the 1950s and 1960s, they instituted their plans. Labor governments imposed environmental regulations on businesses.

Under Prime Minister Clement Attlee, the ruling Labour Party created the tax-funded National Health Service in 1948. The National Health Service was the crowning achievement of a comprehensive welfare program that has been widely described as being "cradle to grave." It made it possible for any British citizen to go to a doctor and get free treatment. Attlee's government also nationalized the Bank of England and a number of industries in order to regulate their growth. These included gas, railroad, electric utilities, coal, and iron and steel industries.

In the 1960s, the Labour Party government under Prime Minister Harold Wilson did not further the aggressive nationalization programs of Attlee. However, Wilson introduced a number of important social reforms. These included the abolishment of the death penalty and the legalization of abortion and homosexuality.

Socialism, as practiced by the Labour Party in Britain, was far removed from what Karl Marx and Friedrich Engels envisioned. Socialism was Britain's utopia. Yet the Labour Party acknowledged that pure Socialism could never be fully achieved. The party also understood that most people would never be able to accept full-scale Socialism as a way of life.

In 1958, English novelist George Orwell wrote a book titled *The Road to Wigan Pier.* He examined why most working people didn't like Socialism. Orwell traveled to an industrial town in northern England. In addition to living with miners, he descended into coal pits. He

Clement Attlee was prime minister of the United Kingdom between 1945 and 1951. He trained as a lawyer, but turned to politics and Socialism after working with children in a slum in London's East End. This photograph shows him addressing a Labour Party conference in Blackpool, England, on June 9, 1945. He was leader of the opposition at the time.

studied people with jobs and people without jobs. Examining class differences in England, he compared the working class and the upper class and discussed why they didn't like each other. Many people saw Socialism as elitist. They didn't like being told what was good for them.

What the Labour Party achieved, then, was a compromise. Throughout Europe, Socialist-influenced governments came to power and thrived. Socialist Léon Blum was the premier of France in 1938 and again in 1946. However, his power was checked by a powerful conservative opposition. It wasn't until the rise of François Mitterrand (1916–1996) in the 1980s that Socialists controlled the presidency, the French Assembly, and local governments.

The Socialism of François Mitterrand

When François Mitterrand was elected president in 1981, his Socialist Party also won a majority in the national assemblies. With the party already in control of cities since the local elections of 1977, Socialists found themselves with a level of control that they had never before had.

Mitterrand began implementing the program of nationalization that he had campaigned on. Between 1981 and 1982, he nationalized twelve of the largest industrial companies by swapping shares for national bonds. The affected industries included telecommunications, chemicals, heavy engineering, aluminum, electronics and appliances, construction materials, and iron and steel. He also nationalized thirty-six banks, and various large finance and insurance companies. Mitterrand also increased workers' wages and shortened working hours.

France's business class reacted sharply to many of these changes. Many chose to remove their capital from France and invest it in other countries. This flight of capital resulted in a significant downturn in the French economy, which in turn forced Mitterrand to change course. Within five years, Mitterrand had lost his clout when conservatives began to exert more control on the government following a string of electoral victories.

The Canadian Experiment

Over the last century, the Liberal Party of Canada has been the most dominant political party in Canada. Since World War II, it has become a champion for progressive social policies. Under William Lyon Mackenzie King (1874–1950), Canada's longest-serving prime minister, the party instituted welfare programs such as mother's allowance and old age pension. Another liberal prime minister, Lester B. Pearson, added universal health care, government-financed

This photograph shows François Mitterrand and Willy Brandt, chairman of the Social Democratic Party of West Germany, during a debate at a meeting of the Socialist International in Paris, France, on September 29, 1978. Mitterrand became the first Socialist president of France in 1981. Brandt was Chancellor of West Germany between 1969 and 1974.

student loans, the Canada Pension Plan, and the Canada Assistance Plan, which provided welfare grants to the nation's provinces. Pierre Trudeau's government promoted bilingualism. It passed the Official Languages Act, which gave French and English equal status in Canada. Trudeau also pushed through a program of multiculturalism, which sought to better integrate immigrants into the Canadian society.

Varieties of Socialism

Sweden initiated broad policies that took care of its citizens from the "cradle to the grave." In addition to a national health care system, Swedish governments have enacted such comprehensive programs as maternity benefits, allowances for children, and pensions. These benefits are paid for by taxes. Germany, too, has Socialist policies, including a nearly universal health care system for its citizens. The United States is one of the only first-world nations that does not have universal health care for its people. President Bill Clinton attempted to introduce major health care legislation in 1993, but failed.

Socialism and the Independence Movements

Throughout the second half of the twentieth centuries, many countries in Africa, Asia, and the West Indies gained their independence from European colonial powers. The leaders of the independence movements, who often led the first independent governments, were attracted to Socialism. Jawaharlal Nehru, for example, tried to boost India's postcolonial economy by borrowing some of the economic features of Stalin's Five Year Plan. He envisioned the Indian population as equal shareholders of the state, which would act as a giant corporation. His plan failed to generate the wealth for which he had hoped. It was further hampered by widespread corruption.

Another variety of Socialist government took root in Africa in the 1960s. It was called villagization. Governments hoped to improve agricultural output by creating villages. In Tanzania, under President Julius Nyerere, who led his nation's movement to independence from England, most of the residents lived in homesteads scattered across the country. After moving them to villages, the economy improved. More important, the country's disparate tribes were united.

But this change had negative side effects too. Under villagization, people used the land differently. While the system was similar to a network of kibbutzim, it often had a bad impact on the environment. Nyerere relented and the government returned to a freer market.

Jawaharlal Nehru became the first prime minister of an independent India on August 15, 1947. He ruled until he died on May 27, 1964. His daughter Indira Gandhi became prime minister in 1966.

CHAPTER FIVE

SOCIALISM IN AMERICA

Eugene Debs, the founder of Industrial Workers of the World, also founded the American Socialist Party.

Karl Marx and Friedrich Engels placed great hope in the United States. In a republic, they expected, the Socialist revolution would take place without violence. Indeed, discontent was brewing among America's industrial workers by the late nineteenth century. They began to organize. First, workers formed small unions. Gradually, the unions began to increase in size and number.

The Wobblies

From the start, there were struggles between worker organizations in the United States. The American Federation of Labor (AFL) was one major group. Another was the Industrial Workers of the World (IWW). Members of this group came to be known as the Wobblies. The groups clashed over many issues. The AFL was composed primarily of craft unions. The IWW had a more industrial base. By 1905, the IWW had emerged as the predominant force in the American labor movement. Its attitude was deeply influenced by *The Communist Manifesto*.

Syndicalism

Led by Eugene Debs, the Wobblies laid out a clear picture of how to achieve its means. It presented its vision of syndicalism in the constitution of the Industrial Workers of the World in Chicago in 1905. The first step would be to form a general union. The union would then create a network of workers spread across the nation.

Gradually, the workers would stage strikes. Eventually, there would be a general strike. The workers would have the power to stop the nation in its tracks. Once they did this, they could negotiate better hours, more humane conditions, and higher pay. Within the framework of the United States, they would reorganize. Instead of the capitalists at the center, the workers would now be in control. Not only would they provide the means for a nonviolent revolution, but they would also establish a structure for the society that would come to exist afterward.

The Fight for Free Speech

After internal struggles, the IWW initiated one of its first national fights in 1907. It was for free speech. A simple way for the group to attract new members was to deliver speeches on street corners.

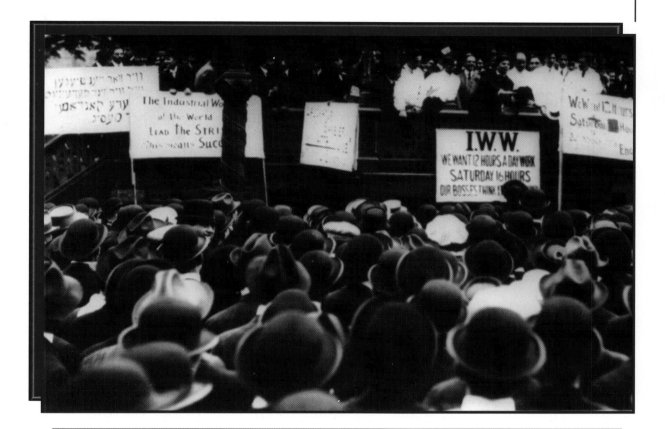

This photograph shows striking barbers at an Industrial Workers of the World demonstration at Union Square in New York City, in May 1913. They were being addressed by Joseph J. Ettor, a firebrand union activist, who led many successful IWW demonstrations throughout the Northeast. IWW and other union activists were frequently honored by local authorities.

Again and again, police harassed the speakers. Despite the fact that the right to gather and speak was protected by the Constitution, many towns passed anti-IWW ordinances. To combat this, hundreds of Wobblies would descend on a town and begin to agitate on dozens of street corners. Police would arrest them. Soon, the jailed Wobblies would overwhelm the town's legal system, and the local government would be forced to repeal the ordinances.

The first major strike the IWW organized took place in the mining town of McKees Rocks, Pennsylvania, in 1907. When factory owners tried to institute a new wage system, a committee of forty workers questioned them. The workers were immediately fired. Quickly, the miners went on strike. For two months, they remained steadfast. They battled state troopers. Several people were killed, and many were injured. Eventually, the company relented and returned to the old wage system.

The IWW's biggest victory took place in Lawrence, Massachusetts, in 1912. Without warning, factory owners cut workers' pay by thirty-two cents a week. In those days, thirty-two cents was enough to buy ten loaves of bread. Word spread quickly.

In less than twenty-four hours, factories throughout Lawrence had called sympathy strikes. The strikes lasted for nine weeks. The battles were vicious. Local police aimed fire hoses filled with freezing water at the picket lines. The more brutal the opposition, the more determined the workers were to continue. In March, nearly three months after the strike began, the employers agreed to give the workers pay raises.

Seeds of Failure

The IWW also won victories in other factory towns, such as Paterson, New Jersey, and Akron, Ohio. Strikes were direct action. Goals could be achieved quickly. Unfortunately, the methods that allowed the IWW such great triumphs also sowed the seeds of their eventual failure. Once the strikes were over, the IWW often failed to

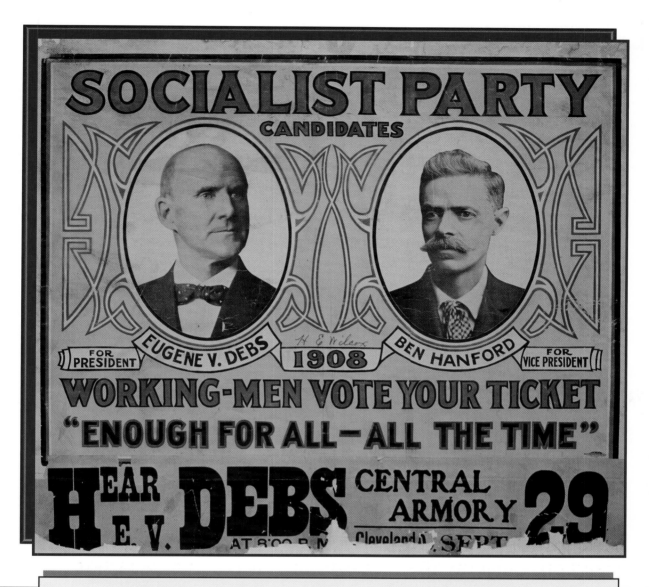

This is a campaign broadside promoting American Socialist Party presidential candidate Eugene Debs. Debs ran for the presidency five times between 1900 and 1920. He was a federal prisoner in 1920 when he made his final run for office. He won more than 915,000 votes.

organize the workers on a more permanent basis. Within a year, there was little union organization left in Lawrence, for example. Still, the influence of the IWW was widespread. It inspired countless local workers to organize.

The Wobblies' Struggle

The existence of the IWW had always been shaky. It was opposed by people and groups on all fronts. From within, great factions formed. Some members of the IWW continued to advocate syndicalism. Others were more inclined toward anarchy. Anarchists distrusted political power. They were suspicious of any attempts to organize on a broad scale. They were also more willing to use violent tactics to achieve their goals. By 1914, the anarchists had alienated many of the left-wing politicians who might otherwise have supported the IWW.

As World War I (1914–1917) loomed, many workers focused their energies on the enemy overseas, forgetting about class struggles on the home front. But the IWW continued to organize strikes. Some IWW members were accused of treason and for being under the influence of the Germans. However, the IWW never made a formal statement against the war.

In September 1917, 165 IWW leaders were arrested and charged with obstruction of the government's war program. The next year, 101 of these men and women were tried and convicted. Their punishments ranged from imprisonment to fines. This was the effective end of the IWW.

Reforms in the United States

As the American government was battling the IWW, the country was entering what became known as the Progressive Era. Many reforms were enacted under Presidents Theodore Roosevelt and Woodrow Wilson. The laws regulated the United States' thriving industries. Companies were becoming huge. They were turning into monopolies, or trusts—vast corporations that cornered the markets, eliminated competition, and controlled prices. While this strategy was good for big companies, it was bad for small companies because they couldn't compete.

Roosevelt became known as a "trust-buster." The Federal Trade Commission was established with the specific purpose of regulating businesses that operated in multiple states. This was only the tip of the iceberg, though. Dozens of laws were passed. The laws did very little to actually change anything on a fundamental level, but they were clearly rooted in Socialist ideals. They were framed with the average citizen in mind.

Journalists called muckrakers began publishing investigative reports in which they revealed the scandalous practices of huge corporations. Author Upton Sinclair's *The Jungle* (1906), for example, looked closely at the meatpacking industry in Chicago. This led to the creation of both the Meat Inspection Act and the Pure Food and Drug Act (1906). The Interstate Commerce Commission was formed as a result of the Mann-Elkins Act when abuses in telephone and telegraph industries were uncovered. The government also began to control the country's money and banking systems more tightly after passing the Federal Reserve Act (1913). Meanwhile, governmental commissions were organized to investigate social ills.

New Laws

Also during the Progressive Era, many states passed laws that placed limits on how many hours a week people were allowed to work. Two constitutional amendments were proposed and passed. The Sixteenth Amendment instituted a graduated income tax. The Seventeenth Amendment allowed citizens to vote for senators in direct elections. Previously they had been chosen by state legislatures.

Though the reforms never went as far as the IWW wanted, they were a start. And they were a direct result of the public uprisings in the early years of the twentieth century. In many ways, these reforms were attempts to keep the Socialist movement under control. President Roosevelt frequently worked in concert with representatives of industry in order to pass laws.

The United States' economy was large and unruly. It was experiencing some of the biggest and most uncontrolled growth spurts it had ever known. Regulation was good for all parties involved. Roosevelt was able to please both the public and big business concerns. These kinds of reforms continued until the beginning of World War II. Their peak came with President Franklin Delano Roosevelt's Works Progress Administration in the late 1930s. His programs distributed money and services to underprivileged people across America. More important, the programs created work for thousands of Americans who were suffering from the effects of the Great Depression.

Socialism never really caught on in the United States. Yet it has influenced various reformers, labor activists, and civil rights activists throughout the twentieth century. However, the excesses of the totalitarian Soviet Union, which emerged as the United States' archrival, led the general American public to equate Socialism with evil and dictatorship. Nevertheless, programs such as welfare, social security, Medicare, Medicaid, and the progressive tax system are examples of how Socialism survives capitalist America. Moreover, the widespread push for universal health care and prescription drug benefits suggest a healthy appetite among Americans for more government-funded assistance programs.

The Future of Socialism

The collapse of the Soviet Union in 1991 and the movement toward democracy and capitalism in its former constituent states seem to suggest that Socialism is in decline. This view is further supported by a trend away from fully centralized economies and nationalization in remaining Socialist/Communist states such as Cuba and China. On the other hand, there is a growing trend within democratic and capitalist societies toward providing—even guaranteeing—social programs, such as universal health care, that are consistent with the Socialist ideal of the welfare state.

Socialism has caused much controversy over the past two centuries. It continues to be debated. There is no question of the powerful impact Socialist theory has had around the world or of its utopian allure.

TIMELINE

1800	Robert Owen sets up model community in New Lanark, Scotland.
1820	Charles Fourier's *Theory of Social Organization* is published.
1847	Karl Marx and Friedrich Engels write and publish *The Communist Manifesto*.
1864	The First International is established.
1867	Marx publishes *Das Kapital*.
1900	The British Labour Party is formed.
1917	Vladimir Lenin rises to power in Russia during the October Revolution.
1922	The Soviet Union is formed.
1928	Joseph Stalin introduces his first Five Year Plan.
1932–1933	Famine sweeps the Ukraine, killing between 6 and 7 million people.
1951	Socialist International issues the Frankfurt Declaration
1956	C. A. R. Crosland's *The Future of Socialism* is published.
1981	François Mitterrand is elected president of France.
1991	The USSR collapses.

Page 21: *The Communist Manifesto* (Excerpt)

The proletariat will use its political supremacy to wrest, by degree, all capital from the bourgeoisie, to centralize all instruments of production in the hands of the state, i.e., of the proletariat organized as the ruling class; and to increase the total productive forces as rapidly as possible.

These measures will, of course, be different in different countries.

Nevertheless, in most advanced countries, the following will be pretty generally applicable.

1. Abolition of property in land and application of all rents of land to public purposes.
2. A heavy progressive or graduated income tax.
3. Abolition of all rights of inheritance.
4. Confiscation of the property of all emigrants and rebels.
5. Centralization of credit in the banks of the state, by means of a national bank with state capital and an exclusive monopoly.
6. Centralization of the means of communication and transport in the hands of the state.
7. Extension of factories and instruments of production owned by the state; the bringing into cultivation of waste lands, and the improvement of the soil generally in accordance with a common plan.
8. Equal obligation of all to work. Establishment of industrial armies, especially for agriculture.
9. Combination of agriculture with manufacturing industries; gradual abolition of all the distinction between town and country by a more equable distribution of the populace over the country.
10. Free education for all children in public schools. Abolition of children's factory labor in its present form. Combination of education with industrial production, etc.

Page 27: *Das Kapital* (Excerpt)

The labour-process, turned into the process by which the capitalist consumes labour-power, exhibits two characteristic phenomena. First, the labourer works under the control of the capitalist to whom his labour belongs; the capitalist taking good care that the work is done in a proper manner, and that the means of production are used with intelligence, so that there is no unnecessary waste of raw material, and no wear and tear of the implements beyond what is necessarily caused by the work.

Secondly, the product is the property of the capitalist and not that of the labourer, its immediate producer. Suppose that a capitalist pays for a day's labour-power at its value; then the right to use that power for a day belongs to him, just as much as the right to use any other commodity, such as a horse that he has hired for the day. To the purchaser of a commodity belongs its use, and the seller of labour-power, by giving his labour, does no more, in reality, than part with the use-value that he has sold. From the instant he steps into the workshop, the use-value of his labour-power, and therefore also its use, which is labour, belongs to the capitalist . . .

Page 33: Addendum to the minutes of Politburo [meeting] No. 93.

In view of the shameful collapse of grain collection in the more remote regions of Ukraine, the Council of People's Commissars and the Central Committee call upon the oblast executive committees and the oblast [party] committees as well as the raion executive committees and the raion [party] committees: to break up the sabotage of grain collection, which has been organized by kulak and counterrevolutionary elements; to liquidate the resistance of some of the rural Communists, who in fact have become the leaders of the sabotage; to eliminate the passivity and complacency toward the saboteurs, incompatible with being a party member; and to ensure, with maximum speed, full and absolute compliance with the plan for grain collection.

The Council of People's Commissars and the Central Committee resolve:

To place the following villages on the black list for overt disruption of the grain collection plan and for malicious sabotage, organized by kulak and counterrevolutionary elements:

1. village of Verbka in Pavlograd raion, Dnepropetrovsk oblast.
5. village of Sviatotroitskoe in Troitsk raion, Odessa oblast.
6. village of Peski in Bashtan raion, Odessa oblast.

The following measures should be undertaken with respect to these villages:
1. Immediate cessation of delivery of goods, complete suspension of cooperative and state trade in the villages, and removal of all available goods from cooperative and state stores.
2. Full prohibition of collective farm trade for both collective farms and collective farmers, and for private farmers.
3. Cessation of any sort of credit and demand for early repayment of credit and other financial obligations.
4. Investigation and purge of all sorts of foreign and hostile elements from cooperative and state institutions, to be carried out by organs of the Workers and Peasants Inspectorate.
5. Investigation and purge of collective farms in these villages, with removal of counter-revolutionary elements and organizers of grain collection disruption.

The Council of People's Commissars and the Central Committee call upon all collective and private farmers who are honest and dedicated to Soviet rule to organize all their efforts for a merciless struggle against kulaks and their accomplices in order to: defeat in their villages the kulak sabotage of grain collection; fulfill honestly and conscientiously their grain collection obligations to the Soviet authorities; and strengthen collective farms.

CHAIRMAN OF THE COUNCIL OF PEOPLE'S COMMISSARS OF THE UKRAINIAN SOVIET SOCIALIST REPUBLIC - V. CHUBAR'.

SECRETARY OF THE CENTRAL COMMITTEE OF THE COMMUNIST PARTY (BOLSHEVIK) OF UKRAINE - S. KOSIOR.

6 December 1932.

GLOSSARY

blacklist A list of people (often created by the government) who should be denied work because of their political or religious beliefs.

bourgeoisie In Marxist theory, the social class that owns the means of production.

capitalism An economic system based on the private ownership of the means of production.

Communism A political system in which all property is shared by its citizens.

direct democracy A political system in which every citizen is a member of the government.

dystopia A state where everything is horrible; the opposite of a utopia.

Fascism A kind of totalitarianism with an emphasis on extreme nationalism.

feudal lord A landowner who, in return for work, protects the farmers living on his land.

genocide A systematic elimination of a group of people based on their religious beliefs or ethnicity.

kibbutz A kind of commune found primarily in Israel.

monopoly A company that controls an industry with no competition.

muckraking A form of journalism designed to expose social injustices.

phalanx A utopian community envisioned by Charles Fourier.

proletariat In Marxist theory, the working class.

serf A farmer working on land owned by a feudal lord.

Socialism A political system in which the means of production is controlled by the workers.

syndicalism A political system in which workers' unions control the means of production.

teleology The study of history by which all events work toward a single goal.

totalitarianism A political system in which a single party rules without opposition.

utopia An ideal state where all people live in harmony.

villagization A form of African Socialism in which farmers were moved from homesteads into small villages.

FOR MORE INFORMATION

Due to the changing nature of Internet links, the Rosen Publishing Group, Inc., has developed an online list of Web sites related to the subject of this book. This site is updated regularly. Please use this link to access the list:

http://www.rosenlinks.com/psps/soci

FOR FURTHER READING

Beecher, Jonathan. *Charles Fourier: The Visionary and His World*. Berkeley, CA: University of California Press, 1987.

Fielding, Steven, ed. *The Labour Party: 'Socialism' and Society Since 1951* (Documents in Contemporary History). New York: Manchester University Press, 1997.

Grant, Neil. Oxford Children's History of the World. New York; Oxford Press, 2002.

Hakim, Joy. *An Age of Extremes* (History of Us). New York: Oxford university Press Childrens Books, 2002.

Renshaw, Patrick. *The Wobblies: The Story of the IWW and Syndicalism in the United States*. Chicago: Ivan R. Dee, 1999.

Ritchie, Nigel. *Communism* (Ideas of the Modern World). Austin, TX: Raintree, Steek Vaughn, 2002.

Zinn, Howard. *A People's History of the United States: 1492–Present*. New York: Perennial Classics, 1999.

BIBLIOGRAPHY

Beecher, Jonathan F. *Charles Fourier: The Visionary and His World*. Berkeley, CA: University of California Press, 1987.

Cowling, Mark, ed. *The Communist Manifesto: New Interpretations*. New York: New York University Press, 1998.

Crosland, C. A. R. *The Future of Socialism*. London: Jonathan Cape, 1956.

Everything2.com. Retrieved January 2003–March 2003 (http://www.everything2.com).

Marx, Karl, and Friedrich Engels. *The Marx-Engels Reader*. New York: W. W. Norton & Company, 1972.

Orwell, George. *The Road to Wigan Pier*. San Diego: Harcourt Brace & Co., 1958.

Renshaw, Patrick. *The Wobblies: The Story of the IWW and Syndicalism in the United States*. Chicago: Ivan R. Dee, 1999.

Wiggerhaus, Rolf. *The Frankfurt School: Its History, Theories, and Political Significance*. Cambridge, MA: MIT Press, 1994.

Zinn, Howard. *A People's History of the United States: 1492–Present*. New York: Perennial Classics, 1999.

PRIMARY SOURCE IMAGE LIST

Page 4–5: Photograph of Clement Attlee addressing demonstrators in Cardiff, England, on August 2, 1936.

Page 8: Engraving of Robert Owen, circa 1810.

Page 10: Engraving of New Lanark, circa 1820.

Page 12: Portrait of Henri de Saint-Simon, circa 1790.

Page 15: Photograph of women working on a Kibbutz in Israel, circa 1935.

Page 18: Engraving of George Ripley, circa 1870.

Page 19: Painting of Friedrich Engels, circa 1860, created by Amsler & Ruthardt.

Page 20: Nineteenth-century painting of Karl Marx by Emil Dreyer.

Page 21: *The Communist Manifesto* by Karl Marx and Friedrich Engels, first English edition, published in London, England, in 1888. Housed at the Karl Marx House in Trier, Germany.

Page 27: *Das Kapital* by Karl Marx, circa 1870.

Page 29: Photograph of Russian construction in Belarus, USSR, on May 9, 1947.

Page 31: Photograph of Americans distributing food from a relief train in Russia in October 1921.

Page 32: Photograph of Vladimir Lenin and Joseph Stalin, 1922. Housed at the Library of Congress Prints and Photographs Division in Washington, D.C.

Page 33: Communist Party memorandum, dated December 6, 1932, regarding grain-collection problems in Ukranian villages. Housed at the Library of Congress in Washington, D.C.

Page 34: Photograph showing political exiles in Siberia, Russia, circa October 1919.

Page 38: Photograph of C. A. R. Crosland, circa 1977.

Page 40: Photograph of Clement Attlee at a Labour Party conference in Blackpool, England, in 1945.

Page 42: Photograph of François Mitterrand and Willy Brandt at the Socialist International Meeting in Paris, France, in 1978. Taken by Richard Melloul.

Page 44: Photograph of Indian prime minister Jawaharlal Nehru during a visit to Indochina in November 1954.

Page 45: Photograph of Eugene Debs, January 1, 1980.

Page 47: Photograph of an IWW demonstration in New York City in May 1913. Housed at the Library of Congress Prints and Photographs Division in Washington, D.C.

Page 49: Campaign broadside for Eugene Debs, 1908. Housed at the Chicago Historical Society in Illinois.

INDEX

PHOTO CREDITS

Cover © AP/Wide World Photos; back cover (top left) NARA; back cover (all others) © The 2000 Nova Corporation; pp. 1 (top left), 38 © Central Press/Hulton/Archive/Getty Images; pp. 1 (top right), 8, 10, 12, 15, 18, 22, 27, 44, 45 © Hulton/Archive/Getty Images; pp. 1 (bottom), 47 © Library of Congress Prints and Photographs Division; pp. 4–5, 31 © Topical Press Agency/Hulton/Archive/Getty Images; p. 19 © Edward Gooch/Hulton/Archive/Getty Images; p. 20 © Archivo Iconografico, S.A./Corbis; p. 21 © Friedrich Ebert Foundation/The Karl Marx House; p. 29 © Bettmann/Corbis; p. 32 © United Press International photo/New York World-Telegram & Sun Collection/Library of Congress; p. 34 © Corbis; p. 33 Library of Congress; p. 36 © Time Life Pictures/Hulton/Archive/Getty Images; p. 40 © Picture Post/Hulton/Archive/Getty Images; p. 42 © Richard Melloul/Corbis Sygma; p. 49 Chicago Historical Society.

ABOUT THE AUTHOR

Jesse Jarnow is a freelance writer who lives in Brooklyn, New York.

Designer: Nelson Sá; **Editor:** Wayne Anderson;
Photo Researcher: Hillary Arnold